A Writer's Guidebook of Facial Expressions and Body Language

S L Lethe

© Copyright 2018 - All rights reserved.

In no way is it legal to duplicate, copy, or transmit any part of this document in either electronic means or in printed format. Recording of this publication is strictly prohibited and any storage of this document is not allowed unless with written permission from the publisher. All rights reserved.

The information provided herein is stated to be truthful and consistent, in that any liability, in terms of negligence or otherwise, by any usage or abuse of any policies, processes, or directions contained within is the solitary and utter responsibility of the recipient reader. Under no circumstances will any legal responsibility or blame be held against the publisher for any reparation, damages, or monetary loss due to the information herein, either directly or indirectly.

Please note the information contained within this document is for educational and entertainment purposes only. Every attempt has been made to provide accurate, up to date and reliable complete information. No warranties of any kind are expressed or implied. Readers acknowledge that the author is not engaging in the rendering of legal, financial, medical, or professional advice.

Table of Contents

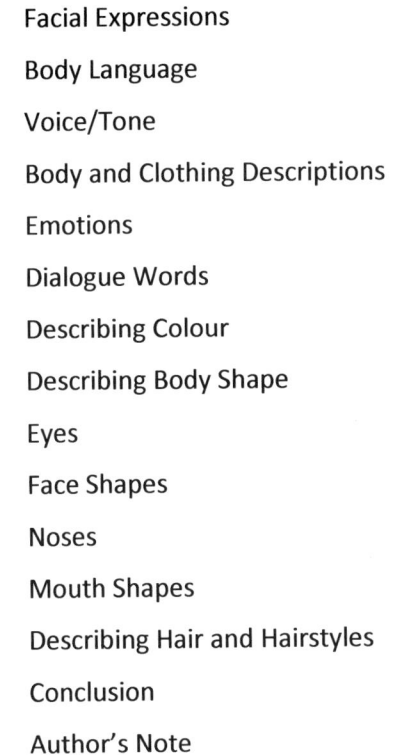

Introduction

Facial Expressions

Body Language

Voice/Tone

Body and Clothing Descriptions

Emotions

Dialogue Words

Describing Colour

Describing Body Shape

Eyes

Face Shapes

Noses

Mouth Shapes

Describing Hair and Hairstyles

Conclusion

Author's Note

Introduction

One of the biggest issues many aspiring (and even established) authors face is how to write facial descriptions and body language. They are essential for readers to paint a picture of how the characters look, how they behave, and what emotions are running through them during the scene. However, as any author will tell you, it is easy to use the same lines over and over again.

This book was created to help address this issue. It is divided into several sections that deal with facial expressions, body language, tone of voice, physical attributes and clothing descriptions, and a section of describing emotions.

In the past, facial descriptions have been my weakest area. I am the author of over 250 books (both fiction and non-fiction and all under various pen names), in a wide range of genres and have worked for a publishing house as a ghost-writer. However, I will still struggle with what my character' faces look like when they are mad or happy or aroused. Several months ago, I began jotting notes down and a short while ago, another author came to me expressing their frustration with the same issue. Thus, this book was created.

The expressions and descriptions below can fit a wide range of genres, from romance to urban fantasy, from sci-fi to horror, and everything else in-between. They can be altered to fit your individual character and story needs. Some of these lines will need you to explain more – who are they looking at? What are they looking at? What is the temperature like? Some are better for dialogue tags instead of facial expressions. You may want to pick a body language that your character does for certain emotions or situations. For example, when one of my main female characters becomes nervous, she twirls a lock of hair around her fingers. Another main character crosses his arms over his chest when he gets scared as a way for him not to show fear in front of others. Both only do these gestures once or twice throughout the book, but it lends them a more depth to their characters. This, in turns, gives the reader and the character more of a connection and enhances the experience.

The section on colours can be used to describe hair, eye, skin colour and clothing. In the past, it was acceptable for authors to describe POC (people of colour) characters with words such as 'chocolate,' 'mocha,' 'cinnamon,' or 'slanted.' These days, however, these food-related terms are not quite as well received and are typically perceived as insulting even if your intention wasn't to. Describing POC characters by way of food is seen as fetishizing and dehumanising. In addition, it is also cliché. As authors, we should always strive for originality.

When describing characters, you can go beyond skin tone. What is the shape of their mouth, their eyes, or their face? Show your readers what the character's body posture is. Are they slumping or standing straight? Perched on the edge of their seat desperately trying not to fidget and failing or sprawled across the floor like a sack of potatoes? You do not, however, have to describe all your character's features at once. Get creative. Use the world around you to help you.

Writing a book is never easy, even for established authors. It is my hope that this book will be useful for you.

Happy writing!

Facial Expressions

- He blinked
- Her eyelids dropped
- She glanced to the ceiling
- She locked eyes with him before they stared back at [third character]
- The grin didn't conjure happiness; it was sinister, hollow, and senseless
- She answered with a hint of a smile on her lips
- The mad woman's eyes glittered
- His left eyebrow shot up
- His eyes bugged
- Tenderness glowed in his eyes
- Her lashes fluttered
- She sized him up
- His eyes scanned her
- A soft smirk of mischief softened by the dimple in his right cheek
- Her smile was plastic, but he didn't notice
- She sneered at him
- His eyes are unusually piercing
- His whole face shimmered with delight
- She could see the veins pumping on his neck/forehead
- An indecipherable look in his eyes
- He doesn't look at me and I can't interpret his face
- She gave him a once-over
- He looked askance at her
- Tears burning in my eyes
- Tears blazing in her eyes
- Tears threatening to spill
- Fighting the tears in her eyes
- Her usually sparkling eyes were dull
- He shook his head, wrinkling his nose
- Her long lashes fluttered, still dotted with tears
- Eyes like a clear blue ocean on a sunny day
- She flushed as she busied herself
- She bit her lip, trying to make her heart stop racing
- Her eyes met his, a hint of competitive challenge in them before she turned back to [*third character*]
- A slight expression of concern on his face
- Her eyes were troubled, but she smiled, trying to hide it
- His blue eyes went cold and appraising
- She fought back a grin at his words
- A thin, almost unnoticeable hint of a smile curved on his lips
- Kaleidoscopic pain dancing in their eyes

- Eyes shaded with terror
- A single sticky tear rolls down her cheek
- Her face tightened instantly
- The regret in his eyes was unmistakable
- A faint smile lined her lips
- He tongues his cheek from the inside
- A tear about to squeeze from her eyes
- The memories curving a weak smile on his face
- His eyes scan her thoroughly
- She pursed her lips as if afraid the truth would spill out against her will
- A seductive gleam flowering in his eyes
- A bitter smile curved her lips
- She tried to smile but her lips felt as rigid and fragile as china
- Her mouth opened and shut and opened again like a fish suffocating in the open air
- His elongated fangs gleaming like polished ivory
- With a feral look in his eyes
- Blue eyes observed his approach
- The colour drained from his face
- He eyed the crowd with a mocking smile
- A wintry smile stretched over her face
- The smile not quite reaching into her wide, dark eyes
- Their expressions a mix of rapture, lust, and fear
- A dazzling smile growing on her face
- A muscle in her jaw twitched
- The smile on her face melted away like ice on a hearth
- Watching her carefully from the corner of his eyes
- His eyes alight with anticipation
- She stuck her nose up in the air
- Her startling dark eyes dancing with merriment
- Her anxiety was betrayed on her otherwise exquisite face
- Their careful eyes scanned the darkness for the merest hint of a threat
- Casting an anxious glance his way
- The disapproving scowl on his face lessened
- His brows knitted together
- A line etched between his brows
- A million questions stormed through his eyes
- Pain sparked in his eyes
- She bit her lip hard around the smile that tugged at her mouth
- The shock on his face lasted only for a second before it disappeared
- Bringing a wistful smile to her face
- Knowing that her smile must look forced and unconvincing
- His eyebrows furrowed in confusion
- The expression on her face was growing distant
- His expression morphed into a frown
- Lifting her chin defiantly
- Her eyes bored into him

- Her eyes shot sparks
- She blinked, tears pooling in her eyes but not spilling over
- The woman's face curled with astonishment and blind rage
- With a saddened look plastered across her face
- His grin evaporated in an instant
- She grinned sadistically as she studied his expression
- She swallowed the scream that rose in her throat
- His lips drew back from gleaming fangs
- She blinked as if just paying attention
- Tears ran down his cheeks, freezing into tiny drops on his face
- A rush of colour crept up his neck, tinting him pink
- Fear danced in his eyes
- His jaw went slack
- Her mouth fell open
- His eyes were dilated
- His pupils flared
- Her eyes swam with tears
- She smiled but it didn't quite reach her eyes
- Her face paled and her eyes glittered dangerously
- The merest hint of uncertainty marred her features
- She closed her eyes, forcing away the tears
- Her eyes had become black shadows in the dimming light
- Fierce determination deepened the lines in his face
- Worry creased the lines in her face
- A lone tear fell from the corner of her eye
- Amazement transformed his face
- They duelled with glares
- Fear and sorrow mingled in her glistening eyes
- Her eyes twinkled with malice
- His eyes seemed fathomless
- His jaw tightened as he tried to reel in his frustration
- A flash of anger shone through his eyes
- Her blue eyes settled on her with concern
- His face took on a grim expression as he shook his head
- A grim expression marring her lovely face
- She found in his eyes a mixture of fury and terror
- Her gaze was misty with tears
- A spark of delight in his beady eyes
- He devoured her with his eyes
- Anger contorted the features of his face
- Understanding dawned on his face
- A triumphant smirk stretched across his face
- He eyed me from head to foot
- He gave her a tired smile when their eyes met
- Delight sparked in her eyes
- She saw him watching her with a strange expression on his face

- He gazed fiercely at her, as if sizing her up
- A fierce heat burned in his eyes
- Sweat beaded on his forehead
- Perspiration shone on her brow
- He regarded her steadily with his green eyes
- He smiled wryly in response, shaking his head slowly
- He seemed unfazed by her brutal honesty
- She saw the first flicker of uncertainty paint his features
- The expression in her eyes changed to something more pensive
- A self-satisfied smile appeared on his face
- Pain flickered in her eyes
- Her face twitched
- Disappointment shrouded his eyes
- His look of determination sent chills through her
- Her eyes became unfocussed
- She watched his expression change to something fierce and dangerous
- Tears stained her cheeks
- A smile tugged at his lips
- Embarrassment reddened her cheeks
- His head tilted down as his eyes bored into hers
- Any sense of amusement slipping from her face
- Her attempt at a smile faltered
- He gave her a sideways glance
- Vacant eyes bore up to the sky
- She tried to smile but the effort never made it past her lips
- A whisper of a smile danced across her lips
- A mischievous grin pinned to his mouth
- He glanced up, his gaze sharp
- A sheepish twitch curled the corner of his mouth
- Shadows passed behind his eyes like a flickering memory
- A heated smoulder in his eyes had her clenching her thighs
- A sceptical frown pulled at his mouth
- A one-sided smile tilting his lips
- A frown locked between his eyebrows
- A question lingered in his eyes
- A resigned sigh puffed between her lips
- His gaze lingered on her lips
- His gaze was a warm caress
- His full lips pressed themselves thin
- He wore an expression she'd never seen before
- A hint of anger danced on his features
- A look of disappointment coated his face
- A lopsided grin adorned his face
- A knot appeared between his brows
- Heat spread through her cheeks
- His grin turned into a full-blown victory smile

- Her soured expression didn't change, but she didn't voice any more objections
- He turned to her with an apologetic look
- She faked a smile
- The right corner of his mouth upturns into a half grin
- Her eyes gleamed with defiance
- His dark eyes widened as they landed on her
- The disappointment was easy to read on her face
- She felt the blood drain from her face
- His face took on a smile of its own
- She turned a sly glance on him
- His face was a manic grin of victory
- She turned to him with a face creased in anger
- He let a small smile pass across his face
- His lashes lowered, shielding his eyes from her
- Relief flooded across her face
- Her full lips trembled her face
- When he looked, some of the sadness had slipped from her face
- For an instant, his gaze darkened
- She cast a desperate glance to the door
- His eyes pierced deep, deep into her own
- His eyes narrowed to slits
- The look of defeat on his face pained me
- His eyes lingered on hers, his expression tormented
- Her lips were upturned in a graceful smile
- A burst of heat lashed at her face
- Her face relaxed into a reassuring smile
- Wielding a seductive smile
- Flashing perfect white teeth
- She chanced a peek at him from beneath her lashes
- A look of horror flashing through his formerly smug gaze
- His nostrils flared in anger
- His soulful dark eyes studied her with an intensity that made her skin melt
- That smile of his turned almost dangerously sexy
- His eyes were heated, and a cocky smile stretched on his lips
- Her blue eyes flashed dangerously
- Her eyes flashed with sheer determination
- A cocky smile claimed his lips
- A strange tension at the corner of his eyes
- Her mouth formed a grim line
- Interest sparks in his gaze
- Her eyebrows pinched
- The worry on her face turned up a notch
- Recognition lit up his blue eyes
- The skin around his eyes crinkled as he smiled
- He could see the argument building in her eyes as they shimmered with defiance
- Her eyes were heavy and grainy

- Her lips twitched as if she had a difficult time hiding her smile
- His lips quirking into a grin
- The sharpness in his gaze
- His eyes remained steady and unblinking on his face
- A deep vertical line pulled between his brows
- Her look lasered to a hawk's predatory gaze
- She offered him a sweeter-than-sugar smile
- I saw recognition in her eyes
- Her smile lost its sincerity
- Her haunted gaze
- His neutral expression mushrooms into something livid
- Slammed brows, pinched lips
- Throwing an understanding smile her way
- Tossing a dark frown at him
- She stared at him, her eyes now more uncertain despite her guarded expression
- The creases lining her face deepened as she smiled
- The small smile on his lips died a slow death
- She concentrated on the act of smiling
- The heat of shame in her face
- A look of childhood wonder crossed his face
- His eyes distant with long memories
- The sadness slips from his face slowly
- He gritted his teeth together
- A slightly panicked look on his face
- His expression shadowed
- She saw something in him unleash
- His eyes glittered as they locked with hers
- A mischievous twinkle in his eyes
- His lips curved up on one side in a wry smile
- A half smile surfaces on my lips
- He stares with interest
- His eyes bulging with revelation
- She looked at him with pursed lips
- Her face was a bubble of hatred and anger
- A menacing smile on her heart-shaped lips gave her real intentions away
- He turned to face her with furious anger in her eyes
- Her eyes smouldering with lust
- She gazed into his eyes as if challenging him to disagree
- Her mouth hardening into a thin line
- His eyes narrowed in mock fierceness
- His face was a mirror of her own
- His smile was shaky but still remained on his face
- Her expression alight with anticipation
- Expressions of pure terror frozen on their faces
- His mouth twisted into a snarl
- His eyes were thrown into shadows

- Her face was set in disapproving lines
- Small lines formed between her eyes
- His eyes looked harsh and distant as a winter's sky
- The relief on her face was painful to watch
- A mocking smile curled his lips
- He fought to keep his face pleasant and blank
- A dawning horror painted his features
- Anger discoloured his face
- A smile shaped his lips
- He frowned at the phrasing
- A vein ticked along his temple

Body Language

- He snaps his fingers
- He wiggled his gloved fingers
- She laced her fingers together as she listened to his words
- She let out an uncontrollable laugh
- She craned her neck and looked at him
- He holds me by the shoulder
- He stands up, slamming his hands on the desk
- She gazed at her watch one more time
- He cupped a hand behind his ear
- She pulled his chin up so he could meet her eyes
- He pushed her away and held her by the arms
- He grips the steering wheel and speeds up
- She rolled her head and walked away
- He balled his hands into fists
- She rested her cheek on her hand and sighed
- He straightened a little as he walked over
- His lips curled but he didn't let go of her hand
- She stepped forward, extending a hand
- She looked over her, cocking her head as she appraised the other woman
- She stepped forward with a lifted chin
- He brought it to his ear
- She bobbed her head
- He jerked his head toward [*insert character's name*]
- She threw her head back
- She bent her knees against her chest and buried her head between them, hugging herself with her own arms
- She closed her eyes, spread her arms sideways, and inhaled all the air she could
- She snaked through the crowd
- He gazed at her for an explanation
- He put his head in his hands
- He covered his eyes with his hand
- She shook the thoughts away
- He clicked his fingers for urgency
- Goosebumps prickled like devil's grass over her skin
- He stopped, as if waiting for her reaction to his suggestion
- He stepped forward, squinting at her face
- She stilled glared, taking a careful step forward
- She stepped forward, hate glimmering from her eyes
- He stops and takes a breath
- She nodded, not even possessing the strength to explain
- She turned around and smiled at his persistence

- She leaned back and smiled with beady eyes
- She rose her head but controlled her temper
- She craned her neck to look at him in surprise
- He nodded twice, saying nothing, looking at his feet
- He turns and dares my eyes
- He nods with closed eyes
- She let out a long sigh
- She hid behind her book
- He lifted his shoulder in a half shrug
- She took a deep breath, her heart racing
- He signalled for her to follow him
- He turned around, anger flushing his face
- Embarrassment staining her cheeks
- Shooting her a suspicious glance
- He shook his head, lips pursed
- He fell onto his knees, head buried in his hands
- She moved with a sinuous grace reminiscent of a dancer
- He thumped his chest with a closed fist
- He shoved the hand aside and turned away
- He reached out to place a comforting hand on her shoulder
- He nodded his head solemnly
- She brushed her palms together
- She rubbed her hands together
- He kept nodding, a smile caressing his lips
- She paused and licked her lips
- He leaned back in his chair, fighting to control his exasperation
- They shared calculating looks
- His head burrowed into the hollow of her neck
- Clasping her hands together with excitement
- Her movements were exquisitely languid, serpentine, and seductive
- His chest rose and fell on ragged breaths
- He made a steeple of his fingers
- Her balance gave out and she slumped in his arms
- She thrashed and twisted but the bindings at her feet and wrists held her fast
- She clenched her teeth
- She tried to gulp air, but her lungs refused to obey
- She stretched out her six-foot frame as far as she could
- She shivered against the chilly gusts of wind at her back
- She crawled backwards on her elbows
- He swiped the legs out from under her
- Her nails bit into his wrist
- She gestured with a thumb
- She extended her middle finger toward him
- She flipped him the bird
- She lifted her gaze, hesitating
- She shook her head in denial

- He opened his mouth to argue, but her fingertips touched his lips and the protest died, unspoken
- She sighed, breath fogging
- Her gave a mock salute
- He drew a finger across his throat
- He pretended to shoot himself in the head
- He flashed her the peace sigh
- He rode forward in a cloud of snow
- He plunged forward in a snarling rush
- He surged on muscled legs
- He fell back in a shower of golden sparks
- He lay in a stunned heap
- Her spine bowing upward as if a string pulled it
- Her eyes were distant with memories
- Shadows of memories danced within her eyes
- Heat rushed up her face
- She shoved/jammed her hands into her pockets
- She glanced at the slow curl of his smile
- Dark eyes stared at her as if she were the proverbial canary
- He blinked at her, his smile slipping around the edges
- His eyes grew distant, as if he were seeing things long ago
- Her chin lifted with an elegance she could never hope to emulate
- She choked back a derisive laugh
- She wrapped her arms around herself
- He extended a hand to her
- She turned her face away
- He sat back on the sofa
- She shifted on her seat
- Her shoulders sagged with disappointment
- He leaned back in his seat, arms crossed over his chest
- She shook her head, not knowing how to articulate what was going on in her head
- He pulled away from her embrace
- He tilted his head to one side, a smirk forming over his face
- He straightened to his full height
- He threw her hands up in surrender
- She blew out a sigh, her shoulders sagging
- She looked at the ground in embarrassment
- She let out a sigh of relief
- A sigh escaped from the confines of her mouth
- A sigh danced on his lips
- A chilling smile rose on his lips
- He massaged the back of his head
- He kneaded his shoulder
- She rubbed her temples
- He threaded a hand through his hair
- He pressed his hand to his forehead and frowned

- She swallowed deeply and blinked several times
- She struggled to keep the tears at bay
- She tugged at her earlobe
- She twisted a lock of hair around her fingers
- She fiddled with her earring
- She bit a nail
- She picked at her nails
- She inspected her fingernails
- He adjusted the lapels of his jacket
- When their eyes met, they found themselves unable to look away
- He continued to hold onto her arm, but loosened his grip
- He moved a step closer, then another, until he stood in front of her
- She struggled to break free, but his arms didn't even budge
- She stood motionless
- With his hand, he captured the back of her head and deepened their kiss
- She kept a poker face and tried to look at him straight in the eye
- He forced her chin upwards
- Her jaw fell open
- His fingers gripped the sides of her face and forced her eyelids open
- Her fingers fluttered in weak protests against his hands trying to fend him off
- He pushed his way through the throng of people
- His brows piqued
- Hands ensnared her from behind
- She ordered herself to climb to her feet
- She picked the lint from her shirt
- He plucked at the cuff of his shirt
- He tugged at his collar
- He adjusted his tie
- Fingers grazed the bottom of her chin, tilting her head up
- He waved a hand in front of her face
- Poised in a battle-ready stance
- His hands cupped her face, forcing her to finally look at her
- His hands ran through her hair, gently brushing the loose strands from her face
- Her nails clawed into his taut muscles
- Goosebumps perforated down her nape
- She bundled her fists into the fabric of his shirt
- He leaned forward and posted his elbows on the table
- It lifted the hairs on his arms
- His thumb skimmed to the corner of her bottom lip then traced the seam
- With one fluid motion
- He pulled her flush to his body
- A visible shudder ran through him
- Beads of sweat clung to his temples
- She crossed her arms over her chest and leaned against the doorframe
- She tucked a wayward strand behind her ear
- She slid down the wall and stared at her feet

- Slowly, she hauled her aching body to her feet
- Strong arms closed around her upper arms and pushed her up, steadying her on her feet
- She stood tall, showing him that she wouldn't budge no matter what
- She let out a long, relieved breath
- He tapped a finger against his lips
- She pressed her fingers to her lips
- She pressed a hand to her throat
- His back hit the floor hard and air flew out of his lungs
- His hands clasped around her waist
- He gripped the hilt of the sword tight
- He took her mouth in a hot and demanding kiss
- She thuds to the ground with a terrible shake
- Warm fingers brushed over her face
- She fidgets with the hem of her shirt
- He pulled her to her feet
- His hands fisted at his sides
- He leaned forward and clasped her by the waist and carefully slid her onto his thighs
- She took a tentative step back
- She sank down on the edge of the bed
- Her arm extended as he brought her palm to his lips
- He folded his hands on his lap
- He cupped the tea in his hands, letting the warmth soak into his flesh
- Her aching legs carried her across the room
- He turned and walked away without waiting for a response
- She bowed low
- He gave a deep sigh of satisfaction as he sipped on the scalding hot beverage
- Sent him crashing to the floor, struggling for breath
- His back foot slipped on the mud
- From the kneeling position on the floor
- He forced his hand to stay away from the hilt of his sword
- His fingers slid over her knuckles
- His thumb brushed against the inside of her palm
- His fingers traced erotic circles on her exposed skin
- His mouth kissed a trail to her other breast
- His fingers closed around her chin
- She hit the ground, her knees slamming into the earth
- She strode down the steps
- Slowly, he reached out to touch her and paused mere inches from her face
- He took her hand in his and studied our entwined fingers
- She hastened her steps
- She set her palms down on the table
- She hooked her feet around the chair legs
- He put his feet up on the desk/table
- She tensed every muscle in her body
- He brushed his knuckles down the side of her face
- She stiffened and jerked back

- She gave a non-committal shrug
- She crossed her ankles in front of her
- She huddled in the corner
- He scanned the crowds for any movement
- Before she could speak, he covered her mouth with his and kissed her
- He grasped her jaw, squeezing it to the point of pain
- Her spine straight as a pencil
- His head whipped around unnaturally fast
- Nodding hard enough to knock something loose
- He cocked his head to one side, listening
- Sweeping long hair out of her face
- He placed one foot in front of the other as though he had forgotten how to walk
- She accepted the offered cup and breathed in the fumes
- He faltered as the old man raised his hand
- She reached forward with outstretched palms
- He hit the floor and rolled without faltering
- He barrelled into him
- His arms collapsed under him
- She fell to the ground
- He held out a hand
- She clasped her hands behind her back
- She squared her shoulders
- He ran his fingers across her hand on the table
- She looked away from him, but his hand caught her chin and forced her to look back
- He placed a hand over hers and gave it a reassuring squeeze before letting go
- He dipped his head slightly
- She clapped a hand over her mouth, suppressing a shriek
- Her phone/keys/bag/knife slipped from her anxious fingers
- Panting in anger and frustration
- She tried to wiggle out of his embracing arms
- He gripped his weapon
- Her hair streamed across her face, blinding her
- Her fingers traced along the hard edges of his jawline
- He peppered the sensitive skin of her wrist with kisses
- His fingers laced through her hair
- He thrust out his chest
- He puffed out his chest
- She whirled around
- She inched forward
- His breath stirred her hair
- His arms flashed forward with deadly speed
- He waved the protests away
- Her fingertips hesitated, hovering just over [insert object]
- She squeezed the [insert object name] until the edges bit into her skin
- Cold fingers curled around her hand
- Her fingertips traced the edges of the wounds

- She clenched her fists and spoke carefully
- He waved it away as if of no importance
- He crept along the wall, hiding in the shadows
- She twisted a lock of her around her fingers
- She drummed her fingers on the table
- His eyes twitched
- He rubbed his thumb over the pads of two fingers
- She swayed on her feet
- He shuffled his feet
- She punched the air
- She pumped a fist in the air

Voice/Tone

- His voice sends a strange shiver to my soul
- He says, breaking the silence
- He says on the other end [of the phone]
- She let out a nervous laugh
- She said in the calmest voice he'd ever heard
- His voice scares me
- His words tick in my head like a time bomb
- A voice sneaked up behind her
- Her words trailed on the air
- The words spill out of her mouth spontaneously
- She said, tears trickling down her cheeks
- The words sprang from her mouth
- [*insert conversation*] her annoying inner voice said
- She said, but her eyes betrayed her reluctance
- She replied on his behalf
- She fired back, not caring about who may be listening
- He says from the corner of his mouth
- She says in a regretful tone
- Her tone brooks no negotiation
- The words flow without having to even think about them
- He asks with horrified eyes
- He asks, still catching his breath
- I don't turn around, but answer as I run
- She said over her shoulder
- Her laughter echoes behind the slammed door
- He retorted testily
- She said, her eyes flashing hope for a brief moment
- He said in a deep voice
- He trailed off, clearing his throat
- She said, hoping her cheeks didn't betray her again
- Yelled at him playfully
- She stifled a laugh at the thought
- She laughed, a sound like tinkling water
- A shattered laugh escaped her lips
- His words rang in her ear again
- [*insert conversation*] her inner voice warned
- He says, not wasting any more time
- She repeated, not knowing what else to say
- His voice is deadly serious
- The words wormed their way through her lips
- He chewed on the words

- His tone is investigative
- He said the words with much admiration as well as resentment
- His tone piques with curiosity
- He hisses between almost-sealed lips
- She hissed through her plastic smile
- Silence stole her breath away
- Her voice resonated behind him
- He says it with all the confidence in the world
- The words force themselves out of my mouth
- She managed to ask, finally
- His warning tone is confident and unmistakable
- With a muttered sob
- With a muffled cry
- His voice fell to whisper on the final word
- He tried to shout, only to discover his voice muffled with terror
- [*insert conversation*] he offered tentatively
- They replied with one voice
- They sang in unison
- He said, hoping he sounded more confident than he felt
- She stammered, groping for words
- Growled a deep voice
- He swallowed hard before answering
- He said, his voice thick with possession
- His words acted as a challenge
- She snapped, anger boiling over
- Amusement dripped from his voice
- But there was no mistaking the fanaticism in his tone
- The predatory smirk in his tone sent a shiver down her spine
- His voice turned dark
- She rasped
- He retorted with an eye roll
- She said, hearing a plaintive note creep into her voice
- She snapped, her lips frothing with spittle
- She finally admitted
- She desperately wanted to say something back
- She suddenly burst out in a nervous, rapid-fire breath
- The threat hung in the air
- There was a bitterness in his voice as his eyes levelled on her
- Her voice was uneasy, almost fearful
- She said, as if it were quite mundane
- Her voice held a warm touch of anger she couldn't control
- His voice held a quiet dignity
- A low growl trickled from his lips
- She uttered with a gravity too real to be faked
- The confident way in which he spoke told her he wasn't accustomed to being disobeyed
- The words came with difficulty

- His tone was stern, making it clear she was about to cross the line
- The truth of his words stung
- The honey-coated words hung in the air
- His voice was hoarse and broken
- The tone of accusation made his temper flare
- She said in what was almost a whisper
- She sounded as if she was wishing it instead of actually believing it
- She didn't miss the lack of conviction in her words
- She could barely force the words out
- She asked, her voice on the verge of breaking
- Her words made me sink in despair
- She rasped out between sobs
- [*insert text*] was all she could manage to say
- She looked confident enough, but her voice broke when she spoke the words
- He responded through gritted teeth
- She couldn't miss the ice in his words
- He whispered in her ear, his breath hot against her skin
- His voice husky with emotion
- She responded, hoping her voice wouldn't break
- He mutters in amazement
- Although she tried to remain calm, there was a faint quiver in her voice
- He scowled, his displeasure clear as day
- His tone brokered no argument
- Each word fell from his lips like thorns digging into her heart
- A gentle tone accompanied his words
- He huffed, sounding uninterested
- He hissed like a hot pain splashed with water
- The words echoed with a lingering hiss
- She choked out
- She whimpered out another plea
- She shrieked, stumbling backwards
- She choked on her own scream
- She whispered in a low, silky voice
- She replied with false pleasantness
- She said on a laugh
- She forced out in a semi-even tone
- She muttered, more to herself than to him
- He said it like it was the last thing he wanted to say
- Her face raised an octave
- His words came out low, tinged with a sensual edge
- His voice was like a net cast into a tumultuous sea
- She said, trying to keep the fear and desperation out of her tone
- Her voice rings out across the room
- She speaks loudly, challenging the room with her words
- A murmur of agreement swirls on the air
- Her voice trills with anger

- With hair the colour of dirty snow
- His eyes were the same colour of the ocean at midnight
- He says with an air of finality
- He spoke softly, ensuring no one else would be privy to their conversation
- But the words died on his tongue
- He allowed some of his frustration to seep into his voice
- She spat out the words like poison
- He forced the admission out between gritted teeth
- He sounded resigned to his fate
- His voice cracked on the last words
- He cursed his choice of words as they left his mouth
- His voice cut through the noise and confusion
- He spoke quietly, the words spilling over each other
- A warning edge entered her tone
- She said, her voice hoarse
- Her voice was heavy with weariness
- A whimper slipped from her lips
- His voice was frantic, wild
- His sensual voice enveloped her like black velvet
- He said through clenched teeth
- She asked, gripped by desperation
- His voice echoed through the depths of her mind
- His voice repeated the words continuously in her mind
- His tone mocking
- He said, steel in his tone
- She said with an air of satisfaction
- Genuine curiosity resonating in his tone
- Laughter bubbled from his throat
- His silky voice lethal
- The moment the words were spoken, everything stopped
- The moment the words left her lips, she wished she could catch them and shove them back down her throat
- He kept his voice level, but she could see it took tremendous effort for him not to yell back at her
- Her tone could have shattered glass
- He cautioned in a low voice
- She could hear the hint of a smile in his voice
- She said, an edge of fear in her voice
- His voice deceptively low and calm
- He blurts the sentence in one breath
- He says, his voice loud enough so everyone hears
- She said, stressing each syllable, hoping he would finally understand
- She moaned theatrically
- Her voice was choked with tears
- She bit off each word, spitting them at him
- She said, surprised by the eagerness in her own voice

- His voice was full of deep pity
- Her voice was still calm, but there was an undercurrent of urgency
- His voice was still calm, but there was an edge of strain to it
- His voice squeezed tight with guilt

Body and Clothing Descriptions

- A strand of black hair dangles on his forehead
- Her face was delicate, heart-shaped with high cheekbones and full parted lips
- His long brown hair waved to his shoulders
- Her lips were dry and cracked
- Her eyes were the colour of pale pearls
- She had an angular face with high cheekbones
- Eyes open no bigger than slits
- A crimson-haired beauty of classical form
- Slender and curvaceous
- With startling blue eyes and a wicked smile
- With a long flowing beard
- Hands that looked as if they could crack walnuts
- Slender and serious
- She possessed a smile that lived within her eyes
- With a waterfall of red hair
- Fine-boned features
- A model of china doll fragility
- With long blonde hair and an angelic smile
- Tall and pale with a shock of white hair
- Eyes the colour of polished jet beneath lashes of spun gold
- He nodded his head, rolls of fat jiggling on his neck as he did so
- His black cloak swirled about his legs like a storm cloud
- Lines of hard-earned wisdom etched the scholar's face
- Her pale features were as smooth and untroubled as a cold mountain lake
- His beard was red as rust
- His black brows winged down
- Dimples adorned his face
- Dark shadows were smeared under her eyes
- High, thin bones shaped his face
- Fanged jaws opened wide to crush his skull
- Her hair was the colour of chestnuts with a deep copper gleam where the sunlight hit it
- His eyes were the colour of storm clouds
- His long hair flew in tangles across his face
- His pupils were the colour and sheen of polished obsidian
- A body full of scars
- A network of scars laced his muscular body
- His long body was clothed all in black
- A black silk shirt clung to his broad shoulders
- Black jeans that outlined his lean legs and hips
- His eyes were so black, so deep, so intense that her body shuddered beneath them
- Not a single strand of black hair lay out of place

- Deep purple patches stained the exposed skin, green hues spreading over the edges before merging into unblemished skin
- His once brown eyes suddenly smouldered into a radiating gold
- The hem of his dark robe whispered over the floor
- Her pale body caked with blood and dirt
- She flashed him a set of bloodstained teeth
- She wore her black curls piled up on her head, some of which had spilled loose over her shoulders
- His shoulders took up the entire width of the doorway
- His black top clung to the hard lines and dips of his torso
- His eyes were a striking contrast to his skin
- Even though his tone was soft as cotton puffs, it felt as though he was yelling
- His perfect white teeth shone against his bronzed skin
- The mid-day sun caught the warm coppery shimmers in her hair
- The colour of his eyes danced between green and blue
- Her long dark hair was a mess of knots
- The muscles in his shoulders were as tight as a violin's string
- Glistening bronze skin
- Smooth alabaster skin and ruby lips
- Intense almond-shaped eyes
- The amount of skin on display was obscene
- His shirt clung to him in all the right places
- Her wine-stained lips
- Filaments of browns, russets, and golds, all the colours of autumn fell like rain through her eyes
- Her eyes were encased in the longest lashes he'd ever seen
- Sweat soaked his clothes
- Her eyes were deep-set and exotically tilted at the corners
- Her cheekbones stretched high
- She was in her late 50's but her smooth coffee-cream skin belied that age
- Dull, blank, exhausted eyes stared back
- Her golden hair streamed out behind her, carried by the wind
- Her hair hung over her shoulders in a myriad of shiny curls
- Straight blades of long black hair that hung like a thick curtain of hair around her delicate heart-shaped face
- High slashing cheekbones
- Luminous brown eyes so dark and deep she felt she was drowning in their depths
- Thick muscles pressed against her back/chest
- Tightly corded muscles
- Dimples dinted his cheeks
- Her the colour of moonlight/starlight
- His face was responsible for conjuring guilty fantasies
- Her long black hair flowed in the wind
- His white shirt rolled up
- An eye-catching silver gown that clung softly to her slender form and dropped all the way to the floor

- Making her look sexy as well as sophisticated
- A deep v-neckline teasing at her cleavage
- Cut into a saucy knee-high spilt at the front to display her leggy figure underneath
- Typically slick and suave
- Wearing a double-breasted black suit jacket and tailored trousers
- Coordinated with a matching black tie
- Effortlessly stylish in a form-fitting black satin dress with glittering embellished sleeves
- She dazzled in a glittering scarlet dress
- Sophisticated with a round-shaped neckline and three-quarter length sleeves before it cut into a daring thigh high spilt at the skirt
- Her hair in loose tousled waves
- With his bowtie stylishly left undone at his neck
- She looked resplendent
- A show-stopping emerald dress featuring a floor-sweeping hem and a square neckline
- The full ballroom style gown injected a dose of added drama
- She swept her locks up into an elegant chignon
- She framed her dark eyes with lashings of mascara
- She completed the look with a slick of pale pink lipstick
- Effortlessly classy in her black floor-length gown
- Her gown fell into soft sheer sleeves
- It flattered her slim figure with a wrap-around ruching across the waist
- She added a slick of pink lipstick in a chic finishing touch
- She was a picture of elegance in a flowing black gown
- Layered beneath a matching sheer kimono jacket
- The outfit was jazzed up by a string of dazzling diamonds across her neck
- Her lilac tea dress was pulled into a high neck and clinched in tightly at the waist
- A dramatic red dress which plunged into a scooped neck before expanding out into a full sequin skirt
- She dazzled in a pleated black dress complete with a saucy sheer mesh top
- His hair curled around his collar in soft waves
- Dark-rimmed eyes
- Her pale face was luminescent in the darkness
- His brown hair swept back in dishevelled waves from his aristocratic face
- Her thick hair spilled around the delicate bones of her face like a raven cloud
- Green eyes glittering like jewels
- His liquid green eyes were calm and smiling
- She was small, dainty
- Her hair falling down her back the colour of autumn-bronzed leaves
- Thick golden-brown hair floated in disarray over her face
- Her black hair was a rich length against the pure white cloth
- Her hair was coiled and wrapped by gold thread
- Scars decorated her bare arms
- She moved with a feline grace that should be impossible to achieve
- The sinful bend of her hips

Emotions

- She felt the anger resurfacing
- His heart sank nervously
- Warmth spread through her
- Her knees wobbled
- Suspicion wafting through her
- A surge of excitement ran through his veins
- Shivers of panic waved like a storm
- Triggering a bittersweet knot of pain in his chest
- Her heartbeat shot to the roof
- An inner feeling drew her towards it
- She didn't want to leave, but something inside her urged her to
- But amidst the confusion and frustration, he …
- Her screams sent shivers of anger down his spine
- A surge of electricity ran through her veins
- A surge of panic
- Pain captured her
- Coldness crept up her spine, fluttering like a breeze through her dress
- His words unwrapping her from her spiderweb of fear
- Fear wrapped itself around her skin like a ghost
- Too many mixed emotions swirled within her chest
- She felt silent anger creep up her veins
- A burning sensation of anticipation in her chest
- Dread slithered through her
- Her throat thickened with sobs
- Pain gripped her chest
- Her breath hitched
- He stole her breath
- Her heart threatened to shatter within the confines of her chest
- Guilt cut at her deep
- Loneliness cut like a blade
- Desperation yanked hard on her, overriding any sense of caution
- Panic tightened at her throat
- Desperation clawing at her
- Relief poured through her
- She battled the urge to recoil
- She suppressed a shudder
- He tasted bile in his mouth
- Her earlier irritation vanished completely
- A sense of foreboding settled in his stomach
- With a growing sense of doom
- Fear and anger burned in her stomach

- Panic flooded her brain
- Her skin crawled
- His stomach revolted
- Her heart swelled, threatening to break free of her ribcage
- She felt terror grasp her throat
- She sank further into bleak despair
- Desire flickered to life
- Every inch of him craved her
- A knot of tension started in her stomach and climbed upward, threatening to choke her
- Fury burst through the fear
- Fear splintered his heart
- Her throat closed with fear
- Fear boiled within her belly
- Fear passed under her skin
- Fear and worry grated at her
- Hope surged within her
- She felt a stab of remorse
- She was struck by an overwhelming sense of loneliness
- Fear, despair, and rage consumed her at once, leaving her unable to think straight
- Dread filled the pit of my stomach
- Desperation coursed through her veins
- Terror exploded within her
- Exhaustion poured through her like waves
- Desire came knocking again hard between her thighs
- Fear rippled through her
- Curiosity clawed at her insides
- That bottomless pit feeling resurfaced in her stomach
- Fury riddled every last nerve
- Anger roared through him
- Rage poisoned his veins
- She was barely able to breathe
- Alarm bells rang in her mind
- The raw agony tore into every fibre of her being
- Fire ran through her veins
- Panic unfurled in his chest
- Her heart was a slow crawl in her chest
- Terror seized her heart and pumped fear into her blood
- Darkness swam in his veins
- Fear grips her into paralysis
- Shame washes over me
- A flood of emotions threatens to rise to the surface
- Fear floods its way down my spine
- Ice slid around his heart
- Fire ignited in his chest
- Her body locked up with rage
- His blood boiled

- Terror trapped the air in his lungs
- Unease stirred in his belly
- Adrenaline pulsed through her
- She felt his anguish like a kick to the stomach
- Grief whispered through her
- Feeling a confidence she didn't really feel
- A knot of emotion burned in her centre
- A thrill of danger went through her
- Her skin crawled with anger
- A small finger of worry jabbed at her chest
- Worry mingled with irritation
- Fear chased over her skin like an icy wave
- Excitement came off her skin in waves
- Fear and dread coiled within his chest
- She tasted her pulse in her throat

Dialogue Words

Writing dialogue is composed of several elements, and how your character says something is just as important as what they say. Additionally, it is important that the reader knows who is saying something. The word 'said' can get boring and repetitive, but using other words can indicate the volume, tone, pitch, and emotion of the character speaking. This will lead to a much more enjoyable experience for the reader.

- Said
- Says
- Supposed
- Thought
- Wondered
- Alleged
- Assumed
- Speculated
- Questioned
- Pondered
- Doubted
- Interrogated
- Quizzed
- Grilled
- Probed
- Queried
- Enquired
- Inquired
- Requested
- Invited
- Bade
- Intreated
- Implored
- Beseeched
- Deliberated
- Entreated
- Considered
- Mused
- Replied
- Grumbled
- Complained
- Groused
- Protested
- Objected

- Responded
- Retorted
- Countered
- Contradicted
- Denied
- Challenged
- Dared
- Tested
- Confirmed
- Disputed
- Refuted
- Contested
- Murmured
- Purred
- Crooned
- Opposed
- Answered
- Muttered
- Slurred
- Garbled
- Roared
- Bellowed
- Bawled
- Hollered
- Yelled
- Screamed
- Screeched
- Squealed
- Howled
- Yowled
- Bayed
- Wailed
- Barked
- Growled
- Snarled
- Yelped
- Argued
- Claimed
- Maintained
- Contended
- Reasoned
- Chided
- Reproached
- Scolded
- Reprimanded
- Chastised

- Rebuked
- Lectured
- Instructed
- Addressed
- Rebuked
- Admonished
- Accused
- Snapped
- Shouted
- Mumbled
- Shrieked
- Groaned
- Moaned
- Whispered
- Begged
- Requested
- Continued
- Cautioned
- Warned
- Demanded
- Commanded
- Ordered
- Directed
- Charged
- Instructed
- Suggested
- Recommended
- Comforted
- Reassured
- Pleaded
- Declared
- Acknowledged
- Stated
- Specified
- Professed
- Vowed
- Swore
- Promised
- Cursed
- Cussed
- Clarified
- Described
- Pronounced
- Explained
- Countered
- Repeated

- Echoed
- Boomed
- Rumbled
- Thundered
- Offered
- Expressed
- Voiced
- Spoke
- Enthused
- Encouraged
- Uttered
- Presented
- Ventured
- Gushed
- Insisted
- Cried
- Blubbered
- Snivelled
- Sniffed
- Whimpered
- Whined
- Droned
- Hummed
- Wept
- Sobbed
- Stammered
- Hesitated
- Spat
- Argued
- Agreed
- Blurted
- Stuttered
- Exclaimed
- Consoled
- Supported
- Gasped
- Gulped
- Swallowed
- Panted
- Wheezed
- Coughed
- Huffed
- Sighed
- Breathed
- Grieved
- Lamented

- Mourned
- Jabbed
- Pointed out
- Sneered
- Scoffed
- Ridiculed
- Derided
- Scorned
- Belittled
- Mocked
- Teased
- Taunted
- Goaded
- Pestered
- Hissed
- Threatened
- Insinuated
- Hinted
- Indicated
- Specified
- Implied
- Glowered
- Glared
- Frowned
- Apologised
- Relented
- Surrendered
- Sympathised
- Commiserated
- Conceded
- Yielded
- Placated
- Calmed
- Mollified
- Soothed
- Assented
- Concurred
- Joked
- Laughed
- Giggled
- Chuckled
- Sniggered
- Tittered
- Guffawed
- Related
- Recounted

- Emphasised
- Recalled
- Resumed
- Concluded
- Raved
- Gambled
- Added
- Enjoined
- Reasoned
- Spouted
- Admitted
- Enunciated
- Sputtered
- Advised
- Commented
- Lied
- Recited
- Squawked
- Affirmed
- Communicated
- Exaggerated
- Complained
- Exclaimed
- Marvelled
- Alleged
- Conceded
- Exhorted
- Mentioned
- Stipulated
- Alluded
- Reiterated
- Stressed
- Exploded
- Mouthed
- Rejoiced
- Confessed
- Related
- Confided
- Surmised
- Appealed
- Faltered
- Consented
- Foretold
- Remembered
- Fretted
- Nagged

- Reminded
- Tattled
- Fumed
- Narrated
- Noted
- Avowed
- Observed
- Reprimanded
- Theorized
- Babbled
- Corrected
- Greeted
- Offered
- Bargained
- Griped
- Phonated
- Retaliated
- Twittered
- Beamed
- Criticised
- Began
- Croaked
- Grunted
- Pledged
- Vented
- Cross-examined
- Belted
- Crowed
- Gurgled
- Vocalised
- Postulated
- Ruminated
- Blared
- Debated
- Hailed
- Prayed
- Sang
- Volunteered
- Bleated
- Decided
- Preached
- Vouched
- Predicted
- Blustered
- Decreed
- Bragged

- Hooted
- Warbled
- Cackled
- Described
- Cajoled
- Dictated
- Inquired
- Called
- Digressed
- Quipped
- Disclosed
- Interjected
- Quoted
- Interrupted
- Raged
- Snickered
- Yammered
- Chanted
- Divulged
- Intoned
- Railed
- Chattered
- Drawled
- Rallied
- Cheered
- Jested
- Rapped
- Sounded
- Sang
- Chimed
- Elaborated
- Accused
- Badgered
- Bickered
- Seethed
- Shot
- Shrilled
- Stormed
- Cooed
- Simpered
- Bleated
- Coaxed
- Guessed
- Gloated
- Imitated
- Lisped

- Stressed
- Went on

Describing Colour

- Ice blue
- Aqua
- Topaz
- Pale blue
- Arctic blue
- Cerulean
- Cobalt
- Azure
- Navy
- Sapphire
- Turquoise
- Lapis-blue
- Electric blue
- Peacock blue
- Ultramarine
- Bleached white
- Snowy
- Lily white
- Snow white
- Milky white
- Off-white
- Diamond
- Bone white
- Blizzard white
- Chalk
- Coconut white
- Linen
- Parchment
- Polar white
- Porcelain
- Virgin white
- Winter white
- Almond
- Ghost white
- Alabaster
- Cream
- Ivory
- Flesh-coloured
- Vanilla
- Creamy
- Amber

- Ecru
- Eggshell
- Fawn
- Hazel
- Beige
- Straw-coloured
- Tawny
- Buff
- Bronze
- Copper
- Brown
- Acorn brown
- Auburn
- Brandy coloured
- Chestnut brown
- Chipmunk brown
- Cider
- Coffee brown
- Cognac
- Cork brown
- Espresso
- Mahogany
- Merlot
- Mocha
- Muddy brown
- Rosewood
- Rust
- Sandstone
- Sienna
- Walnut brown
- Sable
- Whiskey
- Chocolate
- Dark chocolate
- Cinnamon
- Caramel
- Taupe
- Gold
- Molten gold
- Golden
- Ash blonde
- Brassy
- Banana yellow
- Butterscotch
- Custard yellow
- Maize

- Yellow
- Saffron
- Champagne
- Mustard
- Gilded
- Honey blonde
- Strawberry blonde
- Canary yellow
- Starburst yellow
- Lemon
- Sandy
- Brass
- Amethyst
- Boysenberry
- Eggplant
- Heather
- Heliotrope
- Iris
- Raisin
- Wisteria
- Purple
- Lilac
- Lavender
- Magenta
- Mauve
- Plum
- Violet
- Pea green
- Apple green
- Army green
- Basil
- Blue-green
- Cabbage green
- Clover green
- Leprechaun green
- Lime
- Loden
- Sage
- Pine green
- Seafoam
- Teal
- Olive
- Mint
- Avocado green
- Sea green
- Spring green

- Bottle green
- Jade
- Emerald
- Khaki
- Spruce
- Leaden
- Ash
- Ashen
- Silver
- Smoky
- Steel grey
- Grey
- Pearl grey
- Dove grey
- Opal
- Bottle grey
- Flint
- Gunmetal
- Mercury
- Pewter
- Slate
- Wax grey
- Charcoal
- Moonlight
- Starlight
- Platinum
- Corpse grey
- Chrome
- Anthracite
- Coal black
- Ebony
- Onyx
- Obsidian
- Crow black
- Midnight
- Tar black
- Black
- Jet black
- Burgundy
- Crimson
- Scarlet
- Russet
- Wine
- Grape
- Sepia
- Ruby red

- Rose red
- Blood red
- Strawberry red
- Fiery red
- Beet red
- Berry red
- Poppy
- Brick red
- Copper red
- Lobster red
- Claret
- Ruddy
- Bordeaux
- Maroon
- Primrose
- Cerise
- Orchid
- Hot pink
- Baby pink
- Melon pink
- Pale pink
- Rose pink
- Rose gold
- Blush
- Bubble-gum pink
- Cherry-rose
- Cotton-candy pink
- Flamingo pink
- Fuchsia
- Pastel pink
- Cherry-blossom
- Raspberry
- Coral
- Orange
- Mandarin
- Peach
- Calypso orange
- Peachy
- Apricot
- Terracotta
- Umber
- Vermillion
- Ginger
- Burnt orange
- Citrus
- Marigold

- Marmalade
- Pumpkin
- Salmon
- Citrine
- Carnelian
- Bold
- Bright
- Dark
- Pale
- Clear
- Iridescent
- Sparkling
- Light
- Shimmering
- Luminescent
- Brilliant
- Crystalline
- Dull
- Drab
- Glassy
- Translucent
- Transparent
- Glowing
- Twinkling

Describing Body Shape

- Slim
- Slender
- Wiry
- Sinewy
- Underweight
- Skin-and-bone
- Half-starved
- Underfed
- Frail
- Thin
- Reedy
- Malnourished
- Cadaverous
- Scrawny
- Gaunt
- Emaciated
- Small
- Undersized
- Narrow-waisted
- Squinty
- Fat
- Portly
- Tubby
- Pudgy
- Podgy
- Enormous
- Chubby
- Husky
- Plus-sized
- Plump
- Curvy
- Flabby
- Chunky
- Hefty
- Stout
- Overweight
- Athletic
- Hourglass shape
- Lean
- Skinny
- Obese

- Barrel-chested
- Muscular
- Ripped
- Strong
- Beefy
- Big
- Brawny
- Full
- Gangly
- Bullnecked
- Buff
- Burly
- Bulky
- Coltish
- Compact
- Heavy-set
- Lanky
- Long-limbed
- Leggy
- Pigeon-chested
- Tall
- Tiny
- Short
- Average height
- Petite
- Slight
- Round-shouldered
- Solid
- Pear-shaped
- Willowy
- Thickset
- Strapping
- Stooped
- Hunched over
- Stocky
- Ample
- Generous
- Full-figured
- Voluptuous
- Lithe
- Trim
- Bony
- Sturdy
- Ropy
- Strapping
- Powerful

- Toned
- Chiselled
- Broad-shouldered
- Herculean
- Bowlegged
- Bandy
- Swollen
- Thick
- Homely

Eyes

- Almond shaped
- Beady eyed
- Slow eyed
- Wideset
- Close-set
- Cat-eyed
- Squint-eyed/squinty
- Bulging
- Deep-set
- Feline
- Oval
- Round-set
- Shark-like
- Slanted
- Slitted
- Heavy-lidded
- Narrowed
- Hooded
- Angled
- Down-turned eyes
- Protruding
- Monolid
- Up-turned eyes
- Tear-dropped
- Rheumy
- Sunken
- Red-rimmed
- Birdlike
- Catlike
- Jewel-like

Face Shapes

- Oval
- Round
- Heart
- Square
- Rectangular
- Oblong
- Triangular
- Diamond
- Inverted triangular
- Elongated
- Narrow
- Wolfish
- Square jaw
- Chiselled jawline
- Weak chin
- Double chin

Noses

- Roman
- Aquiline
- Bulbous
- Straight
- Narrow
- Hooked
- Crooked
- Snub
- Turned-up
- Dainty
- Button
- Broad
- Long
- Pointed
- Flared
- Fleshy
- Bumpy
- Greek
- Nubian
- East Asian

Mouth Shapes

- Thin
- Full lipped
- Full upper lip
- Full lower lip
- Rosebud
- Pursed
- Wide
- Wide and sensual
- Triangular
- Cupid's bow
- Wide and thin-lipped
- Straight, thin-lipped
- Permanently downcast
- Sardonically lopsided
- Lopsided
- Wide and unsmiling
- Large and sensuous
- Cruel and thin-lipped
- Full and unsmiling
- A rather full and sullen mouth
- Infinitely tempting
- Broad and thin-lipped
- A wide and humorous mouth
- A wide and good-natured mouth
- Crooked
- Sullen
- Scornful
- Passionate
- Sensual
- Unsmiling
- Tight
- Sensitive
- Lush
- Sour
- Dour
- Luscious
- Childish
- Proud
- Slack
- Cruelly sensuous
- Devilish
- Dry

- Cracked
- Chapped
- Moist

Describing Hair and Hairstyles

- Curls
- Locks
- Mane
- Strands
- Threads
- Tresses
- Wig
- Afro
- A cloud-like halo around her face
- Cloudy
- Coils
- Corkscrews
- Dreadlocks
- Natural
- Ringlets
- Kinky
- Texturized
- Jheri curls
- Spirals
- Straight
- Crimped
- Cropped
- Trimmed
- Shoulder-length
- Beehive
- Blunt cut
- Crown braid
- Ducktail
- Curtains
- Bob
- Pixie cut
- Long
- Mid-length
- Braids
- Twists
- Fishtail braid
- French braid
- Frosted tips
- Bantu curls
- Blow outs
- Plaits

- Hi-top fade
- Mop-top
- Razor cut
- Topknot
- Waves
- Blow-dried
- Flat-ironed
- Straightened
- Relaxed
- Pressed
- Hot-combed
- Bald
- Bowl cut
- Shaved
- Man-bun
- Pompadour
- Ponytail
- Buzz-cut
- Clipper-cut
- Flattop
- Pageboy
- Bangs/Fringe
- Coiffure
- Conk
- Finger waved
- French twist/seam
- Kiss curls
- Pageboy
- Poodle cut
- Punk
- Sausage curl
- Shag
- Skin head
- Wedge
- Spit curls
- Comb over
- Combed
- Greased
- Gelled
- Layered
- Moussed
- Pigtails
- Up-do
- Upswept
- Knotted
- A mess of curls piled high

- Bouncy
- Bun
- Bed-head
- Choppy
- Flipped
- Parted
- Mullet
- Mohawk
- Lacklustre
- Oily
- Greasy
- Ruffled
- Straggly
- Tousled
- Wild
- Bushy
- Coarse
- Dense
- Downy
- Fluffy
- Frizzy
- Heavy
- Light
- Fine
- Luxuriant
- Slick
- Sleek
- Porous
- Limp
- Loose
- Tight
- Wispy
- Wiry
- Bleached
- Coloured/dyed
- Bristly
- Groomed
- Highlighted
- Delicate
- Dirty
- Clumpy
- Lacquered
- Slicked-back
- Streaked
- Teased
- Unkempt

- Untidy
- Scorched

Conclusion

When writing, describing how a character looks and sounds adds depth to the reading experience. It is a way for readers to visualise the characters and to set the scene. For many authors, particularly those just setting out on their journey, it can be one of the most difficult aspects of writing.

We've all heard the phrase, *"show, don't tell."* Great dialogue is essential in books but using body language adds more depth since over 50% of human communication is non-verbal. One character's body language can tell another what they are thinking, how they are feeling, and even allows them to anticipate their next move. Body language helps you, as the author, show rather than tell. However, it is possible to overdo it on the showing and too much 'showing' can slow the story down. As with most things, it's about striking the right balance between the two.

The descriptions and dialogue tags in this book are meant to serve as an example but can be used or modified to suit the needs of your book. I've arranged them in this format as I believe it will be easier for you (and myself) to find the right sentence future books as its easy to lose momentum when trying to find the right phrase. Hopefully it will make it easier for you.

Author's Note

If you enjoyed this book or found it helpful, please consider writing a review on Amazon. It doesn't have to be much, a simple 'I liked it,' is enough. You can also find another of my books that may be helpful when writing your novel.

1000 Plot Twists for Your Next Novel

Printed in Great Britain
by Amazon